CATS

CHARTWELL
BOOKS, INC.

CATS

Published by Chartwell Books
A Division of Book Sales Inc.
114 Northfield Avenue
Edison, New Jersey 08837
USA

0-7858-0965-1

This book is produced by
Quantum Books Ltd
6 Blundell Street
London N7 9BH

Project Manager: Rebecca Kingsley
Project Editor: Judith Millidge
Design/Editorial: David Manson
Andy McColm, Maggie Manson

The material in this publication previously appeared in
The Complete Illustrated Guide to the Cat,
An Introduction to Cat Care,
Cat Facts

QUMSPCT
Set in Futura
Reproduced in Singapore by United Graphic Ltd
Printed in Singapore by Star Standard Industries (Pte) Ltd

Contents

MAN'S FELINE FRIEND, 6
Origins of the Cat, 8
Preparing for a New Cat, 10
Providing a Proper Diet, 12
Grooming and Basic Care, 13
Cat Breeds and Types, 14

CAT BREEDS, 16
Longhaired Breeds, 18
Shorthaired Breeds, 38

Index, 64

MAN'S FELINE FRIEND

Cats today are kept as pets in huge numbers all over the world. Curiously enough, their special appeal to humans lies in their great ability to give love, companionship, loyalty and amusement but their independence of spirit and self-sufficiency means that the "untamed" side of their nature is never far below the surface.

Origins of the Cat

Understanding a cat is a question of appreciating the natural instincts which help to direct its behavior. The cat is perfectly adapted to life as a hunter. Its agility, well-coordinated movements and acute senses make it one of the most successful predators in the wild.

THE FIRST CATS

The Miacids were tree-climbing meat-eating creatures. They had a similar dental pattern to that of present-day cats and may also have possessed claws on their feet. The early Miacis was a small weasel-like animal, but they had the necessary brain power and physical attributes to survive and develop further, while other competing groups fell into extinction. As the evolutionary process acted on them about 45–50 million years ago they developed into the ancestors of today's cats

THE HUNTER

Spurred on by their hunting prowess, the cats spread quickly and evolved into many different forms that could take best advantage of their habitat and prey. Most of the early recognizable cats were large and dangerous creatures which have now become extinct such as the fearsome European Cave Lion or Giant Tiger of Asia. Perhaps the most notorious ancestor was the Sabre-Tooth Tiger.

Ancestors of the cat.
Dinictus, about the size of a lynx, existed until 40 million years ago.

Pseudaelurus more closely resembled today's cats until they died out 25 million years ago.

Sole survivor. *The cheetah, is unlike any other cat because it cannot fully retract its claws.*

SABRE-TOOTH TIGER

These tigers were ferocious hunters believed capable of hunting and killing primeval elephants. They used their elongated upper canine teeth for stabbing rather than biting, sinking them deep into their prey. Whilst the Sabre-Tooth line died out leaving no immediate descendants, other smaller animals continued to evolve into today's family of cats, the Felidae.

The Felidae can be divided into three genera.

• *Felis*—from which our domestic cats are descended. These cats purr when they inhale and exhale.

• *Panthera* — big cats such as lions. These cats roar loudly, but only purr during exhalation.

• *Acinonyx*—the cheetah. The only member of its genus. Its claws cannot be fully retracted.

Preparing for a New Cat

As cute and perfect as a kitten may seem, selection of a cat should be based on more than simple emotion. Owning a cat is a long-term responsibility.

CHOOSING A CAT

Before you get a cat, you need to consider whether you want a male or a female, a kitten or an adult. Neutered cats can sometimes be more affectionate and while kittens demand lots of attention they adapt better than an adult to a new home. Longhaired cats require considerable grooming time, if you lead a busy life, perhaps you should choose one with shorthair.

Remember! If your job results in the cat being alone much of the time, then your lifestyle may not be conducive to pet ownership.

The inquisitive, playful kitten is highly appealing, but don't make any hasty decisions.

PLANNING AHEAD

First, make sure your house is safe for the cat. Get rid of toxic plants such as azeleas and rhododendrons. Hide garbage cans, put a guard on your cooker and in front of fires. Make sure cupboards are shut and that any electrical cords and wires are out of reach. Put away ornaments, decorations, sharp or glass objects which may get broken or injure the cat.

Remember! Place wire mesh over fish bowls and baby cots until you are sure the cat considers these beings as part of the family.

WHAT TO BUY

You will need some essentials including a cat bed, a litter box and dishes for food and water. There are numerous types of cat bed available but the polyurethane type filled with old soft blankets is preferable and easy to wash. The bed should be positioned in a warm draft-free place away from the main household traffic. Put the food and water bowls near the bed and make the litter box accessible.

The first trips outdoors should be supervised, otherwise the cat might wander off or take fright and bolt.

Providing a Proper Diet

Cats are carnivores, so when they eat their prey, they eat muscle, skin, bones and internal organs. As a cat owner you should try to replicate that diet, which means supplying a lot of protein and fat.

NUTRITIONAL SCIENCE

Most cats thrive on the scientifically prepared cat foods on the market which are designed to meet their nutritional requirements. Canned foods store easily and have lots of water in them. Water is essential for a cat's diet. Soft moist cat foods also contain suitable fluids, but, if you use dried foods, make sure you provide plenty of extra drinking water as the absence of fluid in these foods can cause bladder problems.

EXPERT DIETARY TIPS

● Don't feed only fish as it can cause vitamin deficiency.

● Don't feed only meat as it produces calcium and vitamin deficiencies.

● Don't give cats raw egg white, it contains avidin which neutralizes biotin.

● Don't give cats dog food. The protein content is not high enough.

Given a well-balanced diet, proper grooming and lots of affection your cat should live a healthy happy life.

Grooming and Basic Care

Grooming should be a regular part of your relationship with your cat. It provides the owner with an opportunity for a close-up check for parasites, minor injuries or other problems.

BRUSHING AND COMBING

Longhaired cats molt all year round, and as a result require twice daily grooming of 15–30 minutes, otherwise their coats will mat. Shorthair cats don't need daily grooming because their coats are easier to manage. They are also more proficient at self-grooming as they have longer tongues. Twice weekly should be sufficient.

PARASITES AND DISORDERS

Cats are susceptible to a variety of diseases, disorders and parasites, some of which can also affect humans. Fleas, ticks, mites, lice and maggots are the major external parasites to look out for during grooming. Check more frequently if your cat seems to be scratching a lot. Regular worming is advised to prevent invasive internal parasites.

In human terms, cats can reach 18 by the end of one year. They start to show signs of old age after 10 years (60 human years). The average life-span is 15 years.

Cat Breeds and Types

Cats have had a checkered history with man. Worshipped in Ancient Egypt and persecuted as agents of Satan during the Middle Ages, they are now kept mainly for their companionship.

BREEDS OF THE WORLD

Cat breed classification varies from country to country. Points of difference center on color and markings, and the length and type of coat. In the United States, the term "Persian" is synonomous with all longhaired breeds except the Angora, Balinese, Birman, Himalayan, Maine Coon and Turkish Van. In Britain, where cats are divided into general categories based on coat length — longhair or short-hair— and origin. All breeds are regarded as either British or Foreign.

HOW MANY BREEDS ARE THERE?

Despite the differences, or maybe because of them in some instances, about 100 pedigree breeds are now recognized. That number reflects duplication as some major organizations classify some breeds differently. All breeds generally fall into one of four categories: Longhaired, Siamese, Shorthaired and Foreign Shorthaired. However that is far from an all-inclusive total.

Some breeds such as the Snowshoe are very new, while others such as the Sphynx and Scottish Fold remain controversial. The 100 breeds that exist today should not be considered the final number. The past few decades have seen th creation of several new ones and there are probably more to come.

SIMPLIFIED APPROACH

In this book we have attempted to overcome inherent problems of worldwide classification by simplifying the categories into Longhaired Breeds and Shorthaired Breeds.

Different colors within a breed are usuly referred to as varieties. Both varieties and breeds normally have capital letter to distinguish them from simple descriptions. For example, "Black Longhair" refers to a particular breed, whereas "longhaired black cat" describes an invidual.

The Himalayan combines the point markings of the Siamese with the body type and coat of the Persian. Recognition of colors varies somewhat between Britain and America.

The appearance of the Blue-Cream British Shorthair differs significantly on opposite sides of the Atlantic. In America, separate areas of blue and cream in the fur are required, whereas British breeders aim to produce cats with mixed, even coloration.

KEY ICONS

A number of key icons are used through the book to provide the reader with at-a-glance reference points.

BODY TYPE

Cats fall into three main body type groupings highlighted through the text with these three cat icons.

 Cobby Compact body, deep chest, short legs and broad head. Large round eyes.

 Muscular Sturdy body, round full-cheeked head.

 Foreign Slender body, long legs. Wedge-shaped head, slanted eyes.

 Grooming The amount of grooming required by each breed. The least needed is graded as 1; the greatest as 4.

 Habitat Indoors The amount of time each breed prefers to spend indoors. Little or no time is graded as 1; most of the time is graded as 4.

 Habitat Outdoors The amount of time each breed prefers to spend outdoors. Little or no time is graded as 1; most of the time is graded as 4.

 Origin The region is shown on the world map with an indicator box.

CAT BREEDS

Longhaired Breeds, 18

Shorthaired Breeds, 38

LONGHAIRED CATS

WHITE PERSIAN

The White is considered to be one of the oldest longhaired breeds and was introduced to Europe from Asia. Of the three forms, Blue-eyed, Orange-eyed and Odd-eyed, the Blue-eyed suffers from deafness. At birth, kittens all have blue eyes. At five weeks of age, a color change may become evident, affecting one or both eyes. The White Persian is a tranquil and sociable cat, but it has a temper and can demand affection.

Origin Europe.
Coat type Thick, dense, silky full frill about neck.
Physique Broad solid cobby type, short thick legs, bushy short tail.
Character Loving, affectionate.
Care Daily grooming.

BLACK PERSIAN

Black Persians were first seen in 1871, at the first British cat show. They are a striking cat with unusual orangish eyes. A true Black Persian is difficult to breed and relatively rare, having flecks of white or rust in their coats.

Origin Europe.
Coat type Silky, thick full shoulder frill.
Physique Cobby type, short thick legs, large round eyes.
Character Loving, prefers indoor life.
Care Daily grooming.

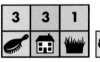

BLUE PERSIAN

Blue Persians were once very fashionable cats to own especially when Queen Victoria acquired one. The exact shade of blue is not an important consideration but any sign of white is a serious fault. Eye color should be orange with no green around the rims.

Origin Europe.
Coat type Silky and thick.
Physique Cobby type, short thick legs, round large paws.
Character Calm, sociable, affectionate, prefers indoor life.
Care Daily grooming.

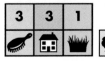

CAMEO PERSIAN

Developed by crossbreeding Smoke and Tortoiseshell Persians. The fur can be one of three varieties: Shell Cameo's fur has very short color tipping of each hair, giving the coat a cloudy appearance; Shaded Cameos have tipping further down the hair to produce a dazzling sheen; Smoke Cameos have very long tips that hide the white undercoat. Varieties include: Cream Shell, Red Shell, Cream Shaded, Red Shaded, Red Smoke, Tabby, Cameo, and Lilac Tortie.

Origin Europe.
Coat type Long, silky, thick.
Physique Stocky, short thick legs, large round paws, rounded ears.
Character Affectionate, sociable.
Care Intensive daily grooming, dry shampoo regularly.

SMOKE PERSIAN

The result of crossbreeding of Black, Blue and Chinchilla Persians. Although the coat appears to be a solid color, the effect is achieved by very long and very dark tipping.The pale undercoat is only visible as the cat moves. There are three varieties: Black Smoke, Blue Smoke and Smoke Tortoiseshell (which is red, cream and black). Generally even tempered, they accept other cats into the household.

Origin Great Britain.
Coat type Dense, thick, silky with a full frill.
Physique Stocky, broad, short thick legs, large round paws, rounded ears.
Character Quiet, home-loving.
Care Daily grooming.

CHINCHILLA PERSIAN

These cats have a sparkling white coat, tipped with black. The tipping occurs most noticeably on the face, at the ears and along the back. When the tipping extends a little further down each hair, producing a silver-gray effect over a white undercoat, the variety is known as Shaded Silver. The thin bone structure and finely tipped fur give the appearance of a delicate creature, but they are generally a healthy and robust cat.

Origin Great Britain.
Coat type Thick, dense.
Physique Broad, solid, cobby type; short thick legs, bushy short tail.
Character Gregarious, placid, affectionate.
Care Daily grooming.

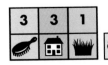

BICOLOR PERSIAN

Originally placed in "any other" class at shows, they now have their own class. Symmetrical patching was the standard but any even patching is now acceptable. A beautiful and contrasting cat, the Bicolor persianfeatures solid colors with white muzzle, chest, undersides, legs and feet. A white frill is now permitted. Varieties include: Cream, Chocolate, Red, Black and Blue.

Origin Europe.
Coat type Thick, dense, silky full frill about neck.
Physique Powerful, solid, broad, short thick legs, bushy short tail.
Character Placid, gentle, good mouser.
Care Daily grooming.

TORTOISESHELL PERSIAN

This is a very rare Persian and difficult to breed, as the genetics result in a cat which will always be female. The cat was produced by the accidental crossing of Persians with non-pedigree, and probably shorthaired, tortoiseshell cats.

Origin Europe.
Coat type Wild looking, thick, dense, silky full frill about neck.
Physique Powerful, massive, short thick legs, bushy short tail.
Character Lively, intelligent, home-loving, affectionate, good mousers.
Care Daily grooming.

CALICO CAT

A female-only variety closely allied to the Tortoiseshell but with the addition of white to the red, cream and black colorings. Known as the Tortoiseshell and White Longhair in Great Britain, where they are very popular.

Origin USA.
Coat type Wild looking, thick, dense, silky full frill about neck.
Physique Powerful, massive, short thick legs, bushy short tail.
Character Lively, intelligent, home-loving, affectionate, good mousers.
Care Daily grooming.

HIMALYAN

These cats are often mistaken for Siamese because the color patterns are similar. They are the product of cross-breeding of Siamese, Birman and Persian in the 1930s, and have the body and coat of a Persian but the point markings of a Siamese. There are seven varieties, with either a cream or ivory body: Blue-Point, Chocolate-Point, Seal-Point, Flame-Point, Lilac-Point, Blue-Cream-Point and Tortoiseshell-Point. Other varieties appear in Britain and all have the sapphire-blue eyes of their Siamese ancestors. Known as the Colorpoint Longhair in Great Britain.

Origin USA.
Coat type Silky, thick, dense with ruff.
Physique Broad, solid, cobby type; short thick legs, bushy short tail.
Character Inquisitive, devoted, playful, happy indoors.
Care Daily brushing.

LILAC KASHMIR

The Lilac Kashmir is a recognized breed in the USA, but in Great Britain it is only accepted as a color variation, known as the Lilac Longhair. They have copper or orange eyes, the thick silky coat of their Persian ancestors but with a pink-gray tint.

Origin USA.
Coat type Fine, silky, thick.
Physique Broad, solid, cobby type; short thick legs, bushy short tail.
Character Curious, active, very affectionate and loyal.
Care Daily grooming.

CHOCOLATE-TORTOISESHELL PERSIAN

Developed during the selective breeding for Himalayans, the Chocolate-Tortoiseshell Persian has only recently been admitted to show status. They are active cats and are happiest when doing something.

Origin USA.
Coat type Dense, silky.
Physique Broad, solid, cobby type; short thick legs, bushy short tail.
Character Curious, active, very affectionate.
Care Daily brushing.

BIRMAN

Also known as the Sacred Cat of Burma, the Birman is believed to have lived in Buddhist temples in Burma. It has a white or pale tinted coat with darker points, white-tipped front paws, and white-gloved rear paws. There are four widely accepted varieties: Seal-Point Birman, a pale golden coat and brown points; Lilac-Point Birman, off-white body and pink-gray points; Blue-Point Birman, blue-white coat and blue-gray points; and Chocolate-Point Birman, yellow-white coat and milk-chocolate points.

Origin Burma.
Coat type Fine, silky, longer on neck and tail.
Physique Long body, narrow face, medium length legs, heavy whiskers.
Character Affectionate, even-tempered, gentle.
Care Regular grooming.

BALINESE

A longhaired Siamese, the Balinese first appeared as a longhaired mutation in a litter of Siamese kittens in the 1950s. There is no connection with Bali beyond the name. By comparison to other Persians, the coat of the Balinese is relatively short. They have the manners of the Siamese and the slender body and sapphire-blue eyes but with a longer coat. There are a number of varieties: Seal-Point, Blue-Point, Chocolate-Point, Lilac-Point, Red-Point, Cream-Point and all the tortoiseshell and tabby variations.

Origin USA.
Coat type Medium length with no undercoat or ruff.
Physique Long muscled body, long legs, small egg-shaped paws.
Character Affectionate, demanding of affection, aloof, athletic.

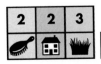

2	2	3

TURKISH ANGORA

These cats were the first longhaired breeds to be introduced into Europe in the 16th century. They were imported from the Turkish city of Angora, now known as Ankara. Several varieties of the Angora are recognized: Brown Tabby, brown coat with black marking; White, traditional color and orange, blue, or odd eyes; Calico, white coat with black and red patches and orange eyes; Blue, with orange eyes; Black Smoke, white coat with black tips and orange eyes; Silver Tabby, silver coat with black marking and green or hazel eyes; Cinnamon; Blue Tabby, blue-white coat with blue marking and orange eyes.

Origin Turkey.
Coat type Silky, medium length, thicker on underside, tail and neck. Sheds extensively in warm months.
Physique Long, slender body, long thin legs, forelegs shorter than hindlegs.
Character One-person cat, gentle, playful.
Care Daily brushing and combing especially when moulting.

MAINE COON

This distinctive breed developed from American farm cat stock is the result of crossings of non-pedigree shorthairs and Angoras. The Maine Coon needs lots of open space, enjoys the comforts of home but must have access to a garden as they like an active romp outdoors. Possibly due to its wild origins, they are happy to sleep anywhere. Any of the standard colors and patterns are acceptable in this breed, with the exception of Chocolate-Point, Lilac-Point and Siamese.

Origin USA.
Coat type Very thick, shaggy.
Physique Large muscular body, large tufted ears, large eyes, long tail.
Character Amiable, amusing, agile. Enjoys activities outside and inside.
Care Daily brushing to maintain its thick coat in good condition.

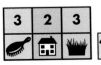

SOMALI

The Somali is a longhaired mutation of the Abyssinian and was first bred in the USA in the 1960s. They have a "wild" appearance but the graceful body structure of the Oriental breeds. There are three varieties: Sorrel or Red Somali, red-brown ticked with bands of chocolate-brown; Usual or Ruddy Somali, brown ticked with bands of darker brown or black; Blue Somali, blue-gray ticked with bands of darker version of the same. They are intelligent cats eager to learn tricks quickly but love freedom and grow restless when confined indoors. This is not a good indoor cat.

Origin USA.
Coat type Medium length, soft, silky.
Physique Long slender body, slightly arched back.
Character Gentle, soft-voiced, athletic, cautious.
Care Regular brushing with a soft brush.

2	1	3

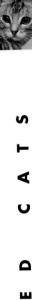

CYMRIC

A longhaired version of the Manx, the Cymric first appeared in Canada in the 1960s in litters of pedigreed cats that had no longhaired animals in their ancestry. Their name comes from the Celtic word for Wales, off whose shores the home of the Manx, the Isle of Man, lies. All colors and patterns are acceptable. The length of tail can vary widely. Some cats have a remnant tail and are known as "Stumpies", while those which have nearly full tails are called "Longies".

Origin Canada.
Coat type Long, thick undercoat, shiny smooth top hairs.
Physique Stocky, muscular build, hind legs are longer than front legs, arched appearance.
Character Affectionate, intelligent, good mousers, compatible with other animals.
Care Regular brushing with a soft brush.

2	2	2

JAVANESE

During the breeding programme for the Balinese to expand their color ranges, those colors which were not acceptable for the Siamese were grouped together to form a separate breed — the Javanese. It is a very active cat preferring outdoor life to the comforts of home. The varieties so far include the Cream-Point, Red-Point, Blue-Cream-Point, Tortoiseshell-Point, Lilac-Cream-Point, any of these colors in tabby markings on the points, is called Lynx-Point in the USA.

Origin USA.
Coat type Long, silky, no under-coat.
Physique Long thin body, medium-length tail, almond-shaped slanted eyes.
Character Active, acrobatic, climber, jumper, affectionate, vocal.
Care Regular brushing with a soft brush required.

2	1	3

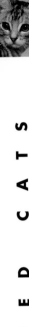

NORWEGIAN FOREST CAT

This is an ancient cat breed, hardy and accustomed to outdoor life hunting for its own food. They must have space to roam and explore, and are happiest when involved in an activity, such as mousing at which they are proficient. Their features resemble the Maine Coon Cat, although the two are separate breeds. Varieties include: Brown Tabby, Bicolor Blue-and-White, Tortoiseshell, Blue-Cream, Red Smoke, Bicolor Black-and-White.

Origin Norway.
Coat type Long, water-resistant, outer coat, woolly undercoat. Sheds once a year.
Physique Heavy body, thick strong legs, heavy whiskers, thickly furred tail.
Character Hardy outdoor breed, good hunter, agile climber, enjoys human company.
Care Only occasional combing.

TIFFANY

A shaggy longhaired mutation of the Burmese, the Tiffany retains the seal-brown coloring of the former. The kittens do not display this longhaired quality at birth. The Tiffany is loving of its owner and new acquaintances, but is demanding of praise, attention and play time. They enjoy travel and the view from the car window. The Tiffany is an able mouser but is happy indoors, living a long life of up to 18 years.

Origin USA.
Coat type Long, thick, silky.
Physique Strong muscular body, long shaggy tail, almond shaped eyes which should be yellow-gold in color.
Character Friendly, self-confident, humorous, enjoys travel, adaptable.
Care Daily brushing.

TURKISH VAN

The Turkish Van is an Angora Cat, first imported into Great Britain in 1955, and officially recognized there in 1969. It is not recognized in the USA. The cats bred near water generally enjoy swimming and as such are easy to bathe. The Turkish Van has been a house cat for many centuries and is affectionate towards the whole family. They are extremely intelligent but not very active. They molt extensively in the summer, assuming a virtually short-haired appearance, but the coat grows back rapidly as winter approaches.

Origin Turkey.
Coat type Long, soft, silky no undercoat. White blaze down forehead.
Physique Muscular, full and long, small round feet, large tufted ears.
Character Gentle, affectionate, enjoys water, not active preferring life indoors.
Care Daily brushing especially during the summer molting period.

RAGDOLL

The Ragdoll originated in California and is rare outside the USA. They get their name from their ability to relax completely when picked up so that they become floppy, like a ragdoll. The typical posture of the Ragdoll is lying flat on its side and completely relaxed. They have an equal liking for indoor and outdoor life. They have an extremely high tolerance to pain and an overly mild nature. Varieties include: Bicolor, Colorpoint, Mitted.

Origin USA.
Coat type Long, full.
Physique Long solid body, medium-legs, large round paws.
Character Docile, enjoys quiet, goes limp when picked up.
Care Regular brushing required with a soft brush to maintain the long coat in good condition.

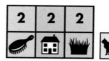

BRITISH SHORTHAIR

A naturally occurring type of cat in Great Britain, the British Shorthair was refined at the end of the 19th century. These muscular cats are very adaptable but appear happiest when allowed some time outdoors. They make excellent pets for the family requiring little care as they are extremely self-sufficient. There are many varieties, sharing the same general characteristics: White, Black, Cream, Blue, Blue-Cream, Classic Red Tabby, Mackerel, Tortoiseshell, Tortie-and-White, Smoke, Tipped.

Origin Great Britain.
Coat type Short but dense.
Physique Stocky body, short muscular legs, short tail, large round ears.
Character Excellent family pet, easy to look after, intelligent.
Care Easy to groom. Requires little care.

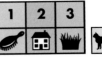

BRITISH SPOTTED SHORTHAIR

A version of the British Shorthair, the British Spotted is often referred to as "Spottie". They have the same pattern as the Mackerel Tabby British Shorthair but with the stripes broken up into spots. It has an extremely wild look, resembling the coats of some of the wild cats. This resemblance is echoed by its healthy muscular body and its willingness to catch mice. There are four popular varieties: Silver, Red, Brown and Blue.

Origin Great Britain.
Coat type Short dense fur.
Physique Stocky muscular body, muscular legs, short tapered tail.
Character Healthy, strong, smart, skilled mouser, adaptable.
Care Fur should be rubbed with a gloved hand occasionally.

BRITISH BICOLOR SHORTHAIR

The true pedigree of this cat is far from common. The standard for Bicolors requires that the color is well defined and evenly distributed. Not more than two-thirds of the cat's coat should be colored, and not more than half should be white. There are four recognized varieties: British Cream-and-White, British Orange-and-White, British Black-and-White, and British Blue-and-White. All have copper or orange eyes.

Origin Great Britain.
Coat type Short but dense.
Physique Stocky, short muscular legs, short tapered tail, large round paws.
Character Healthy, hardy, independent, skilled mouser, child friendly.
Care Occasional rub with a gloved hand.

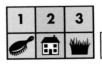

MANX

The true origins of this cat are steeped in folklore. The most likely is that cats of the Spanish Armada, which sank off the Isle of Man, found their way ashore. The truncated Manx tail results from an incomplete gene. There are three tail varieties: Rumpies (with only a hollow where the tail should be), Stumpies, Riser or Stubbies (with a residual tail), and Longies (with a certain amount of tail).

Origin Great Britain.
Coat type Double, with thick short undercoat and longer overcoat.
Physique Stocky body, powerful legs, forelegs shorter than hind legs.
Character Friendly, intelligent, easy to train, good hunter, long lived.
Care Gentle brushing required occasionally.

AMERICAN SHORTHAIR

Like its British cousin, the American Shorthair is very much a cat of the streets and the countryside. They were brought to North America with the European settlers. Once ashore, they interbred and adapted to the new environment. Larger and more muscular than the British Shorthair, they have a hardy and healthy nature. There are nearly 30 color varieties recognized including: White odd-eyed, Black with gold eyes, Cream with orange eyes, Silver Tabby, Red Bicolor and Shaded Silver.

Origin USA.
Coat type Thick and dense.
Physique Athletic and strong, powerful large paws, large round eyes.
Character Skilled hunter, hardy, resistant to cold, enjoys outdoors, loving.
Care Easy to groom.

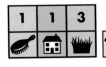

AMERICAN WIREHAIR

At first glance, the American Wirehair looks like any other shorthaired cat. But on close inspection, the hair feels wiry and coarse to the touch and springs back when stroked. They originate from a mutation in a litter where one kitten had a thin wiry coat. The hair was studied and shown to be unlike other cats such as the Rexes. The kitten and a littermate were bred and produced further wiry-coated kittens which were named after the Wirehaired Terrier. Varieties are similar to the American Shorthair with the exception of the patched tabby pattern.

Origin USA.
Coat type Dense, curly, woolly, coarse.
Physique Athletic, powerful, large round paws, males larger than females.
Character Alert, inquisitive, independent, affectionate, adaptable.
Care Occasional brushing of their wiry spring coat required.

EXOTIC SHORTHAIR

A descendant of the American Shorthair but a man-made breed. Through selective breeding, this new breed was created to carry the dignified character of the Persian but with the shorter, easier-to-care-for coat of the American Shorthair. Burmese were also used in the breeding for a brief period. They have an ideal nature for family life being affectionate with children. In all the varieties, the eye coloring must complement the coat.

Origin USA.
Coat type Dense, plush, medium length.
Physique Short low-set body, short thick legs, short bushy tail, large paws.
Character Placid, affectionate nature, ideal family pet.
Care Gentle brushing required occasionally.

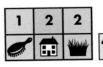

SIAMESE

This is the one breed of cat that is instantly recognizable by nearly everyone. No other coloring is as universally familiar as the classic Seal-Point Siamese. An extrovert cat, the Siamese love to have visitors in the home but their personality is unpredictable. In the USA there are four recognized breeds: Seal-Point, Chocolate Point, Blue-Point and Lilac-Point. In Great Britain, the Tabby-Points, Tortie-Tabby-Points, Tortie-Points, Red-Points, and Cream-Points are also officially recognized as Siamese. In the USA these varieties are classed as a separate breed: the Colorpoint Shorthairs (see p.46).

Origin Far East.
Coat type Short, very soft and fine.
Physique Thin slender body, long thin legs, small paws, large ears.
Character Strong personality, demanding, jealous of other animals with an unpredictable wild streak to its nature.
Care Daily brushing.

COLORPOINT SHORTHAIR

In Great Britain, the varieties of this breed are officially considered to be Siamese cats, but they are classed as a separate breed in the USA. They were produced by mating Siamese cats with other breeds, such as Abyssinians. The Colorpoint shares the characteristics of the Siamese, having the same loud voice and acrobatic traits. Varieties include: Cream-Point, Cream, Lynx-Point, Red-Lynx-Point, Chocolate Tortoiseshell-Point, Lilac-Tortoiseshell-Point, Blue-Tortoiseshell-Point.

Origin USA.
Coat Type Short, soft, fine.
Physique Slender thin body, long thin legs, almond-shaped slanted eyes, large pointed ears.
Character Can be taught to walk on a lead, jealous of other animals, vocal, extrovert.
Care Daily brushing.

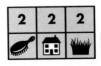

RUSSIAN BLUE

The breed probably originated in the Russian port city of Archangel and was brought into Great Britain aboard a Russian merchant ship. They have also been known by the names Maltese and Spanish Blue. A white variety was produced for a time in Great Britain, but dropped from breeding efforts due to lack of interest. It is now very rare.

Origin Russia.
Coat Type Fur resembles that of a plush covered toy. A heavy undercoat gives the fur a sheen of mink.
Physique Slender muscular body, long tail, oval eyes.
Character Quiet, shy, indoor cat.
Care Regular brushing.

KORAT

This is a rare breed in its native Thailand, where they are often given as wedding gifts to bring prosperity and good fortune. These cats do not like street noises and get easily upset at noise.

Origin Thailand.
Coat Type Short thick silky.
Physique Stocky muscular body, medium tail, large prominent eyes.
Character Quiet, affectionate, intelligent. playful, inquisitive.
Care Daily grooming and precautions against viral respiratory infections.

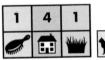

ABYSSINIAN

These cats are believed to be descended from sacred Temple cats of Ancient Egypt. They have a ticked coat and are striking cats with huge eyes. Varieties include: Ruddy, Red and Blue, Chocolate, Lilac, Fawn, Silver, Sorrel/Silver and Blue/Silver.

Origin Ethiopia.
Coat Type Short and glossy, dark fur.
Physique Lithe, sleek, slim legs, long tail, prominent erect ears.
Character Climbers, intelligent, playful.
Care Daily exercise and play, groom with a gloved hand.

FOREIGN OR ORIENTAL SHORTHAIR

These cats are a solid color variation of the Siamese. They were created by breeders who found that their solid-color Siamese cats were excluded from Siamese categories. Each color is considered as its own breed. In Great Britain, the Foreign Black is not recognized as a separate breed; only (Lilacs) Lavenders and Whites are accepted. In the USA, a wider range of colours are recognized and the various colors are divided into five classes: Solid, Shaded, Smoke, Tabby, and Bi-(Parti) Color.

Origin Thailand.
Coat Type Short, very soft, fine.
Physique Thin, slender body, long legs, small paws, triangular head, large pointed ears.
Character Like the Siamese, demands total devotion, enjoys traveling, can walk on a lead, vocal.
Care Need lots of play and exercise, daily grooming to remove dead hairs.

2 1 3

HAVANA

These cats originate from Great Britain although their name suggests Cuban beginnings. They are a man-made breed and are the result of a selective breeding programme of the Siamese without its point pattern. They are named after the cigar, of which color it approximates, but for a while the name Chestnut Brown was used when their British origins were under suspicion. This is a one-color breed, but show standards differ between the USA and Britain.

Origin Great Britain.
Coat Type Short, glossy and even.
Physique Long thin body, long thin legs, small paws, extremely large ears.
Character Intelligent, playful, affectionate, loyal. Enjoys an equal amount of indoor and outdoor activity.
Care Daily grooming with a gloved hand.

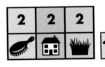

BURMESE

Nearly all of today's Burmese are descended from the mating of a single queen who was imported into the USA and crossed with a Siamese tom. Varieties include: Brown (Sable in USA), Chocolate (Brown in USA), Blue, Lilac, Platinum. All have gold to yellow eyes. In Britain, the whole range of Tortoiseshell variations are recognized. There is also a Red Burmese, the result of crossbreeding. The coloring is lighter than in other reds.

Origin Thailand.
Coat Type Short and satiny.
Physique Medium length body, muscular, forelegs longer than hindlegs, round head.
Character Enjoys human company, affectionate, happy indoors or out, likes plenty of play and exercise, long-lived.
Care Daily grooming with a gloved hand.

JAPANESE BOBTAIL

The Japanese Bobtail is a unique breed. Its name is derived from the short tail of only four or five inches in length, which is curled, with hair growing out of it in all directions, producing a fluffy, bobbed look. Its muscular body belies the fact that this cat prefers the cosy indoor life and family affection. The Mi-Ke is the most popular variety (black, red and white, or calico). Other varieties include: Black, White, Red, Black-and-White, Red-and-White, and Tortoiseshell

Origin Japan.
Coat Type Soft and silky.
Physique Slender, muscled, long legs, triangular head, slanted oval eyes.
Character Ideal family pet, affectionate, vocal, suited to an indoor life.
Care Light daily brushing to maintain the condition of the coat.

SINGAPURA

In its native Singapore, this cat is referred to as the "Drain Cat", a name that reflects their low status. As a result of limited human contact, they have a reserved temperament. With care and gentle handling, they will come to love human company. They are adaptable cats but prefer an indoor, peaceful existence. There are many naturally occurring varieties in Singapore, but only ivory ticked with brown, and a white-and-ticked tabby bicolour have been seen in the USA.

Origin Singapore.
Coat Type Short and silky.
Physique Small body with a constant slight arch to the back, round head, large ears.
Character Placid, undemanding, reserved, adaptable.
Care Stroking with a gloved hand, keeps the coat in good condition.

1	3	1

BOMBAY

The Bombay is a man-made breed which originated in the USA in the 1970s. It has been produced by cross-breeding Burmese and American Shorthairs. The name refers to the dark coated panther, native to India, after whose city of Bombay the cat derives it's name. This is a single color breed. They are indoor cats, never needing to spend time outdoors, as they detest loud noises and prefer a sedate life. They are therefore suitable cats for those homes which are unoccupied during the day.

Origin USA.
Coat Type Short and close lying, with a sheen looking like patent leather.
Physique Medium body and legs, round head, strong chin, copper eyes.
Character Affectionate, placid, dislikes noise.
Care Occasional stroking with a gloved hand maintains the glossy coat.

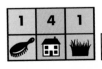

TONKINESE

One of the newest breeds, the Tonkinese originates from Canada in the 1970s, the result of a cross between Siamese and Burmese parents. They have point markings similar to the Siamese, but much less defined. They are one of the most affectionate cats and travel well. There are five varieties: Natural Mink, Blue Mink, Honey Mink, Champagne Mink, Platinum Mink, All have blue-green eyes.

Origin Canada.
Coat Type Short, soft and shiny fur with a glossy sheen.
Physique Medium sized body, long legs, large ears.
Character Outgoing, affectionate, playful, adaptable, travels well. Prefers outdoor life.
Care Rubbing with a gloved hand keeps the coat shiny.

SNOWSHOE

The Snowshoe is the result of a cross between the Siamese and the American Shorthair, no show standard has been set up as the breed is very recent. Siamese like, the Snowshoe has two varieties so far: Seal-Point, with fawn coat with a paler chest and underside, seal-brown points, and snow white paws; Blue-Point, with blue-white coat with a paler chest and underside, gray-blue points, and snow white paws. The eyes are deep blue.

Origin USA.
Coat Type Short, soft, glossy.
Physique Slender, muscular, thin legs, triangular head, large rounded ears.
Character Affectionate, enjoys indoor life, active.
Care Groom by stroking with a gloved hand.

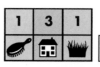

REX

There are actually two breeds of this cat: the Cornish Rex (right) and the Devon Rex (left). The Devon Rex has the habit of wagging its tail like a dog when happy and combined with the curly coat has the nickname of "Poodle Cat". All colors and patterns are recognized in both Rexes, with the exception of Bicolor in the Devon; in the Cornish asymmetrical white markings are allowed. Those with Siamese point patterns are referred to as Si-Rex.

Origin Great Britain.
Coat Type Cornish: curly, silky. Devon: curlier, coarser and thinner.
Physique Long, slender, arch in the back, curl in the tail, wedge-shaped head, large pointed ears.
Character Inquisitive, extrovert.
Care Protection is needed in cold weather as the coat is fine. Groom by stroking with a gloved hand.

1	3	1

EGYPTIAN MAU

Cats similar to the Egyptian Mau are depicted in art that dates back to 1400 B.C. in Egypt. A cousin of the Abyssinian, they are reputed to be direct descendants of the sacred Temple cats. They are a naturally occurring breed in Egypt. There are four varieties: Smoke, Silver, Bronze, Pewter. All should have a scarab beetle pattern on their brows. They are adaptable and enjoy indoor and outdoor activites.

Origin Egypt.
Coat Type Dense fur, finely textured.
Physique Medium muscular body, triangular head, large pointed ears.
Character Lively, affectionate, able mouser but happy indoors.
Care Needs protection from the cold, groom with a gloved hand.

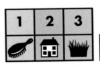

SPHYNX

The most unusual breed of cat. Unlike every other breed, they are hairless and quite rare. Organizations which recognize the Sphynx accept it in any color and pattern, with eye color complementing the coat color. Varieties include: Black, Siamese, Red, Tabby, Blue-and-Cream, Blue Bicolor. Although the Sphynx is unhappy being handled too much, it does like people and prefers the warm indoors to the colder weather outside.

Origin Canada.
Coat Type Down-like hair that feels like suede.
Physique Long slender body, long tapered tail, long legs, very large, very pointed ears.
Character Sociable, dislikes being handled, indoor cat.
Care Needs a warm environment.

EUROPEAN SHORTHAIR

Resembling the British Shorthair, the European Shorthair has developed from the natural shorthair, popular in many European homes. The breed is generally territorial and combative towards other cats and has a definite need to roam large, open spaces. There are many varieties of the European Shorthair including: White, Red, Tortoiseshell, Brown Tabby, Tortoiseshell-and-White.

Origin Europe.
Coat Type Short, thick, finely textured.
Physique Muscular, sturdy, round head, small ears.
Character Friendly, outgoing, territorial, intolerant of other cats, hardy.
Care Regular brushing with a gloved hand.

2	1	4

SCOTTISH FOLD

The breed gets its name from a litter where several cats were born with folded ears in 1961, in Scotland. The breed is not officially recognized in Britain because of the potential hearing problems caused by the forward folding ears. They are fully recognized in the USA. There are many varieties including: Cream with orange eyes; Black Smoke; Silver Tabby; Blue-Cream; Red Bicolor. Kittens do not reveal whether they have inherited the folded ears until their first month of life.

Origin Great Britain.
Coat Type Short, dense and soft.
Physique Short rounded body, short muscular legs, ears folded forward.
Character Very affectionate, tolerant of other pets, hardy, able mouser.
Care Brush regularly. Check and clean the ears regularly.

2	2	3

MALAYAN

This is a very recent breed, originating in the USA, officially recognized in 1980. They differ from the Burmese only in color and are classed as a Burmese in Great Britain. Malayan kittens are regularly and naturally produced as part of Burmese litters. There are three varieties: Blue, Platinum, Champagne. All have yellow eyes. They are adaptable but much prefer living indoors.

Origin USA.
Coat Type Short, fine.
Physique Stocky muscular body, large rounded ears, muscular legs.
Character Friendly, outgoing, loves attention, adaptable, dislikes loud noises.
Care Groom by stroking with a gloved hand.

OCICAT

The breed takes its name from the wild Ocelot; both have a dark, spotted coat. To achieve this look, the Ocicat was bred from pedigree Abyssinians, Siamese and American Shorthairs. The Ocicat is larger and heavier than other Oriental breeds. They are active cats and need outdoor periods and plenty of play when indoors. They are able to walk on a lead like a dog. Their coat is cream-gray with irregular brown markings throughout.

Origin USA.
Coat Type Short and thick.
Physique Large muscular body, muscular legs, large paws, very large, pointed ears.
Character Active, acrobatic, can be walked on a lead, needs access outdoors.

Index

Abyssinian 48
American Shorthair 42
American Wirehair 43

Balinese 28
Bicolor Persian 23
Birman 27
Black Persian 19
Blue Persian 19
Bombay 54
British Bicolor Shorthair 40
British Shorthair 38
British Spotted Shorthair 39
Burmese 51

Calico Cat 25
Cameo Persian 20
Cheetah 9
Chinchilla Persian 22
Chocolate-Tortoiseshell Persian 26
Colorpoint Persian 25
Colorpoint Shorthair 46
Cornish Rex 57
Cymric 32

Devon Rex 57
Dinictus 8

Egyptian Mau 58
European Shorthair 60
Exotic Shorthair 44

Foreign Shorthair 49

Grooming and basic care 13

Havana 50
Himalayan 25

Japanese Bobtail 52
Javanese 33

Korat 48

Lavender Kashmir 26
Lilac Longhair 26

Maine Coon 30
Malayan 62
Manx 41
Miacid 8

Norwegian Forest Cat 34

Ocicat 63
Oriental Shorthair 49
Origins of the cat 8–9

Preparing for a new cat 10–11
Providing a proper c 12
Pseudaelurus 8

Ragdoll 37
Rex 57
Russian Blue 47

Sabre-Tooth Tiger 9
Sacred Cat of Burma 27
Scottish Fold 61
Siamese 45
Singapura 53
Smoke Persian 21
Snowshoe 56
Somali 31
Sphynx 59

Tiffany 35
Tonkinese 55
Tortoiseshell Persian 24
Tortoiseshell & White Longhair 24
Turkish Angora 29
Turkish Van 36

White Persian 18

INDEX